Traditional Hymns

Complements All Piano Methods

Table of Contents

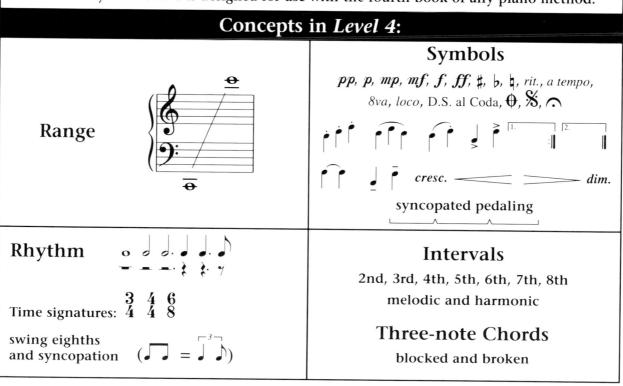

Traditional Hymns Level 4 is designed for use with the fourth book of any piano method.

Concepts in *Level 4:*

Range

Symbols

pp, p, mp, mf, f, ff, ♯, ♭, ♮, *rit., a tempo, 8va, loco,* D.S. al Coda, ⊕, 𝄋, ⌢

cresc. ⟨⟩ *dim.*

syncopated pedaling

Rhythm

Time signatures: 3/4 4/4 6/8

swing eighths and syncopation

Intervals

2nd, 3rd, 4th, 5th, 6th, 7th, 8th melodic and harmonic

Three-note Chords

blocked and broken

ISBN 978-0-634-03680-4

HAL • LEONARD CORPORATION

7777 W. BLUEMOUND RD. P.O. BOX 13819 MILWAUKEE, WI 53213

Visit Hal Leonard Online at
www.halleonard.com

Every Time I Feel The Spirit

African-American Spiritual
Arranged by Fred Kern

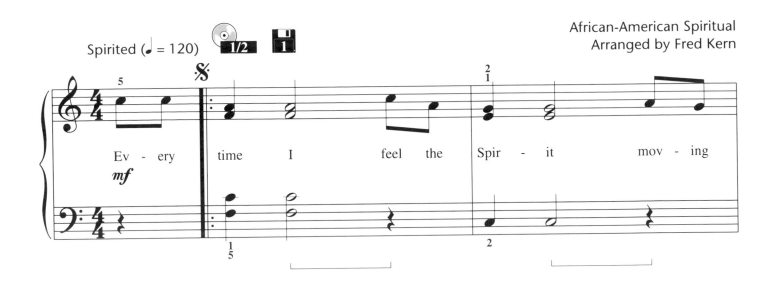

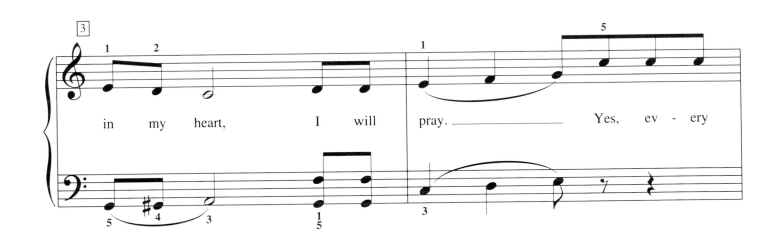

CODA

D.S. al Coda

3

God Will Take Care Of You

Words by Civilla D. Martin
Music by W. Stillman Martin
Arranged by Phillip Keveren

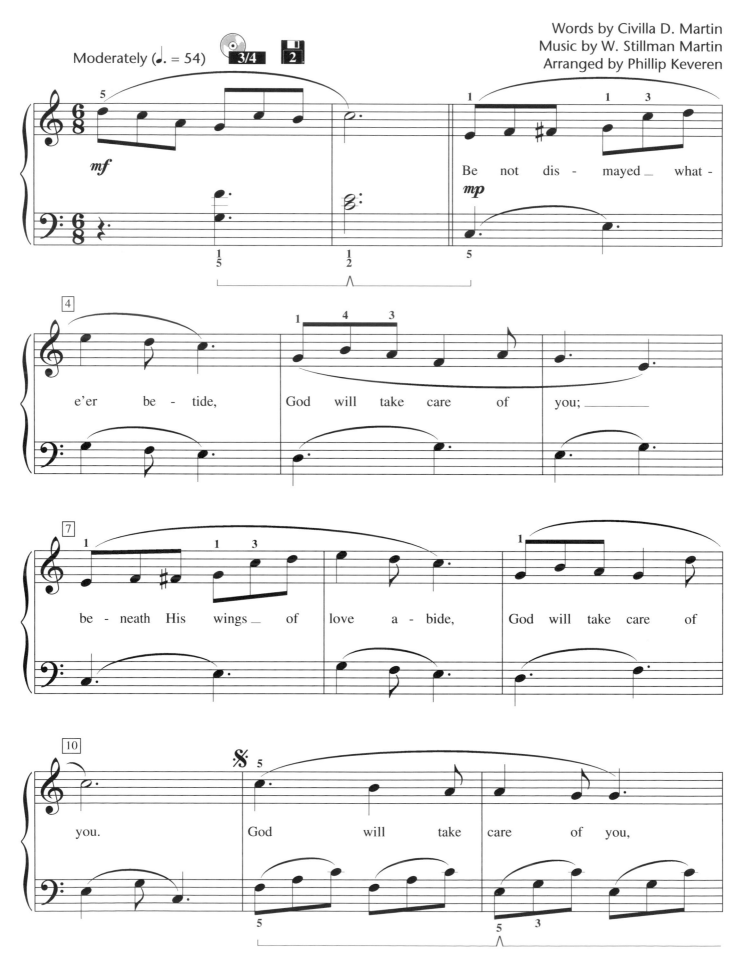

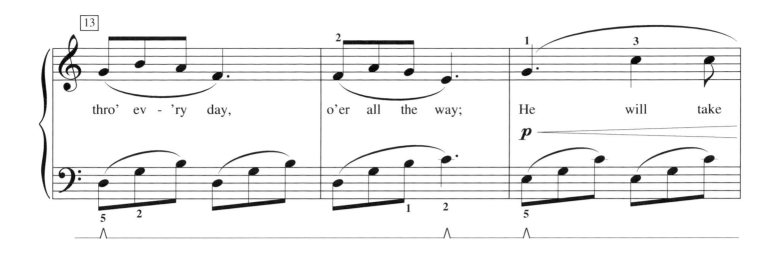

thro' ev -'ry day, o'er all the way; He will take

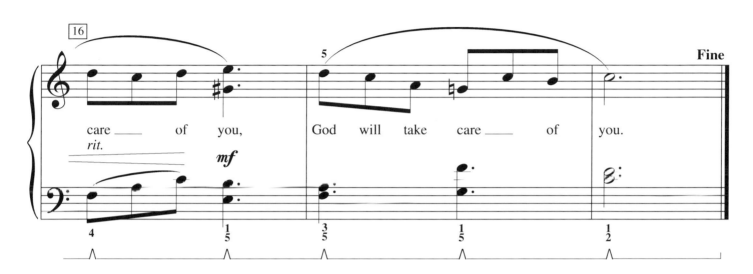

care ___ of you, God will take care ___ of you.

Fine

Thro' days of toil ___ when heart doth fail, God will take care of you. ___

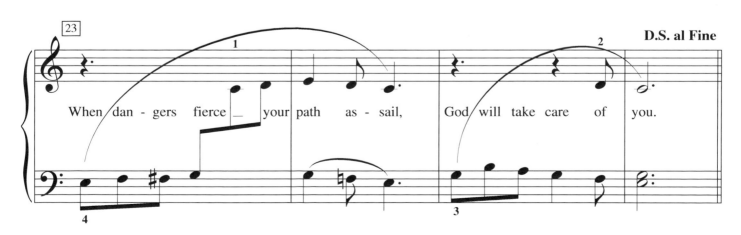

When dan - gers fierce ___ your path as - sail, God will take care of you.

D.S. al Fine

5

In Christ There Is No East Or West

Words by John Oxenham
Music by Alexander Robert Reinagle
Arranged by Mona Rejino

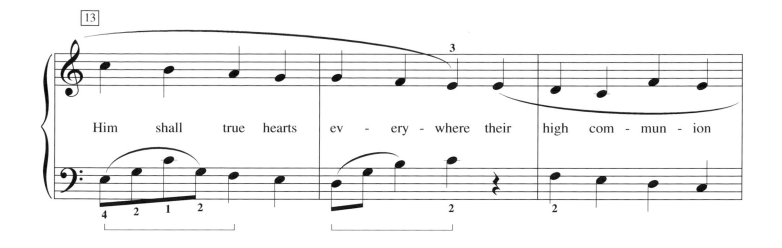

Him shall true hearts ev - ery - where their high com - mun - ion

find; His ser - vice is the gol - den cord close -

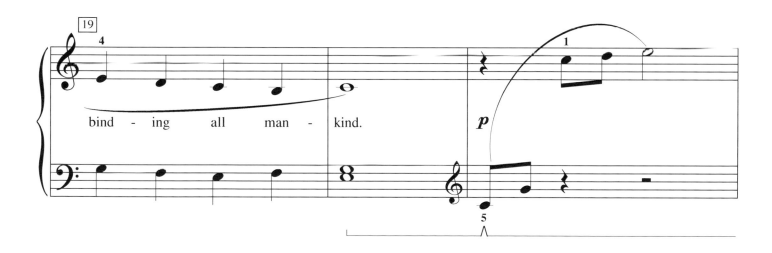

bind - ing all man - kind.

p

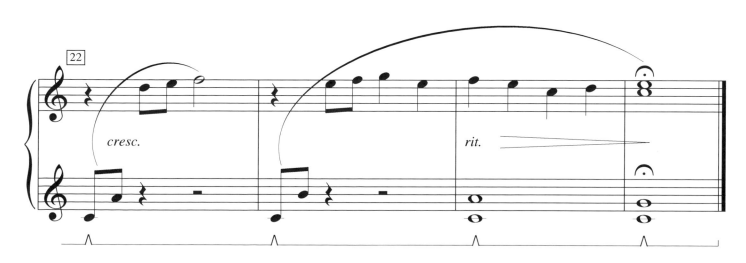

cresc. *rit.*

Lord, I Want To Be A Christian

Traditional Spiritual
Arranged by Mona Rejino

heart, in my heart, in my heart, in my heart. Lord, I

want to be a Chris - tian in my heart.

rit.

9

My Faith Looks Up To Thee

Words by Ray Palmer
Music by Lowell Mason
Arranged by Fred Kern

take all my guilt a - way,

O let me from this day be

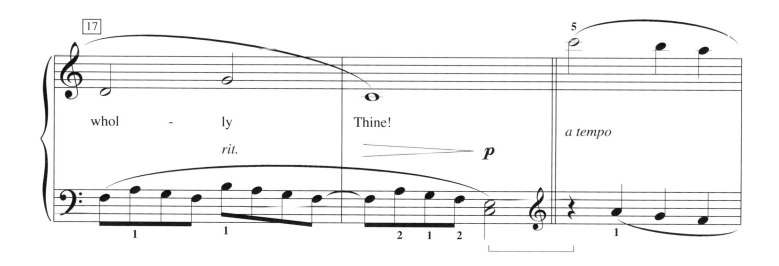

whol - ly Thine!

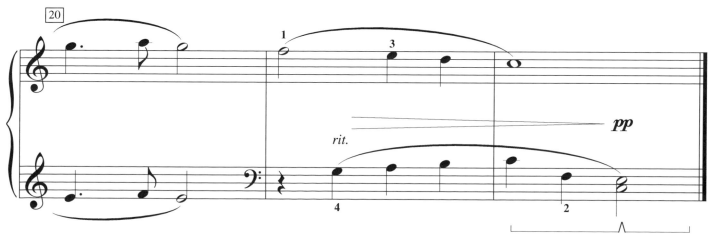

11

Nobody Knows The Trouble I've Seen

Soulfully, with great freedom (♩ = 76)

African-American Spiritual
Arranged by Phillip Keveren

13

Once To Every Man And Nation

Words by James Russell Lowell
Music by Thomas J. Williams
Arranged by Fred Kern

* Can be played:

for the ___ goal or e - vil side;
and up ___ on ___ the throne ___ be wrong:

some great ___ cause, some
yet that ___ scaf - fold

new de - ci - sion,
sways the ___ fu - ture,

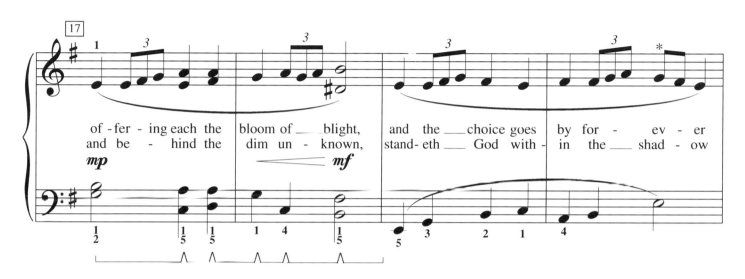

of -fer -ing each the
and be - hind the

bloom of ___ blight,
dim un - known,

and the ___ choice goes
stand- eth ___ God with-

by for - ev - er
in the ___ shad - ow

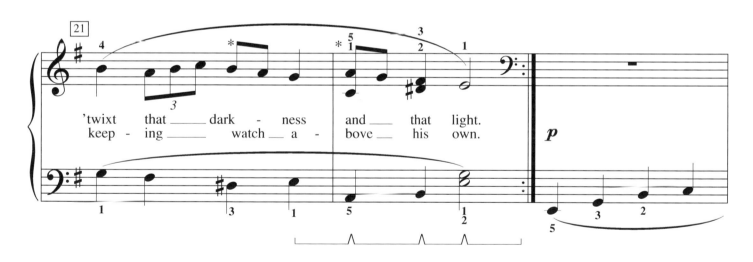

'twixt that ___ dark - ness
keep - ing ___ watch ___ a -

and ___ that light.
bove ___ his own.

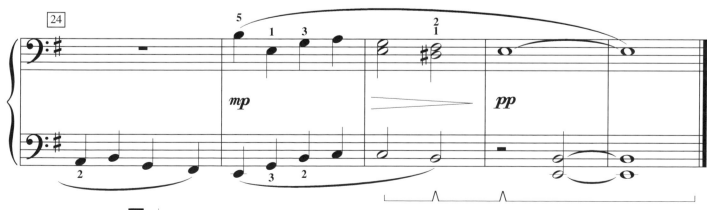

Can be played:

15

Praise To The Lord, The Almighty

Words by Joachim Neander
Translated by Catherine Winkworth
Music from Erneuerten Gesangbuch
Arranged by Mona Rejino

With gladness (♩ = 112)

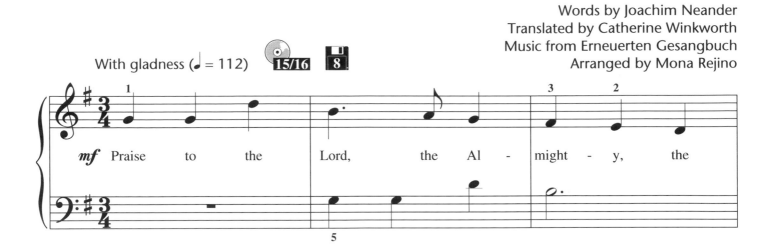

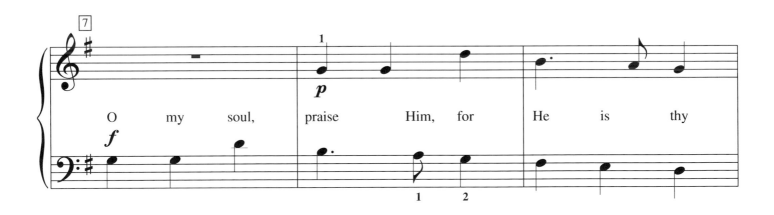

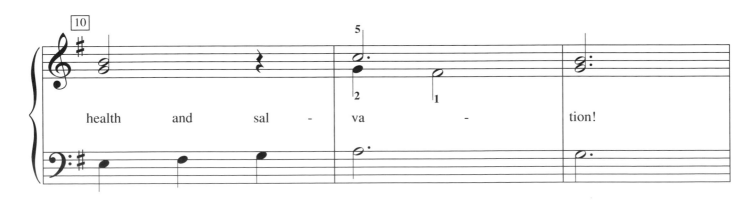

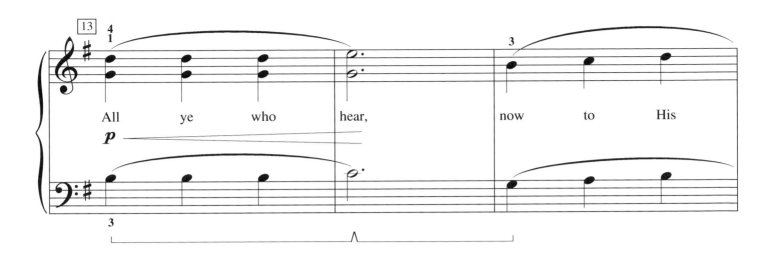

All   ye   who   hear,   now   to   His

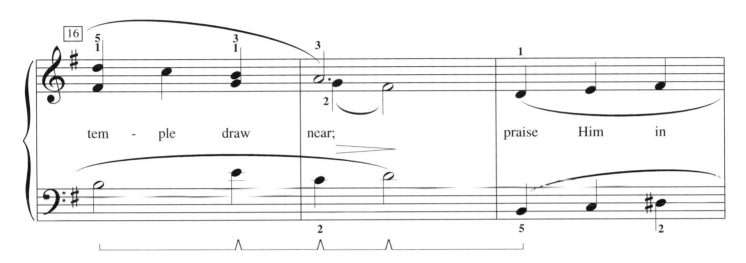

tem - ple   draw   near;   praise   Him   in

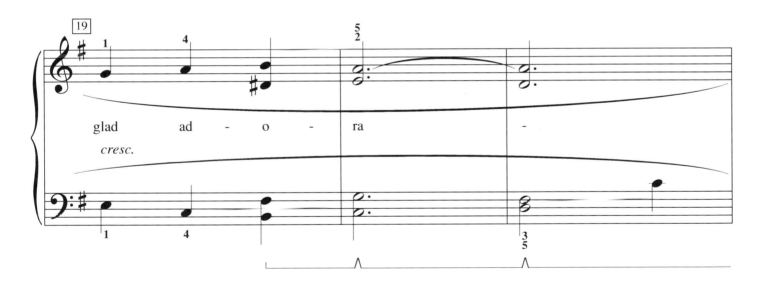

glad   ad - o - ra   -

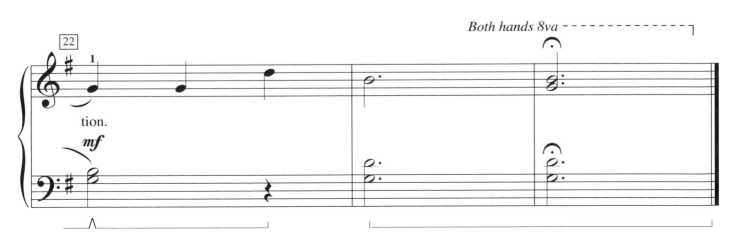

tion.

Both hands 8va

17

This Is My Father's World

Words by Maltbie D. Babcock
Music by Franklin L. Sheppard
Arranged by Mona Rejino

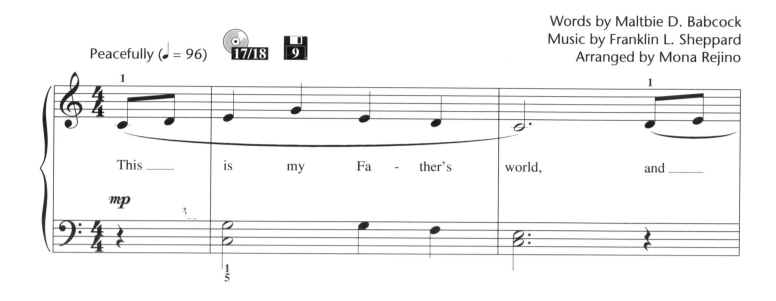

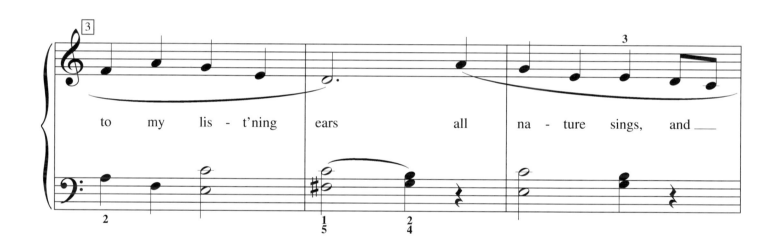

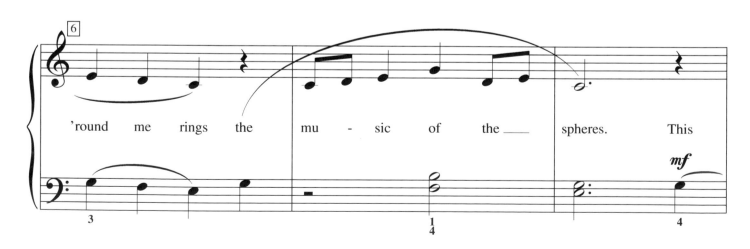

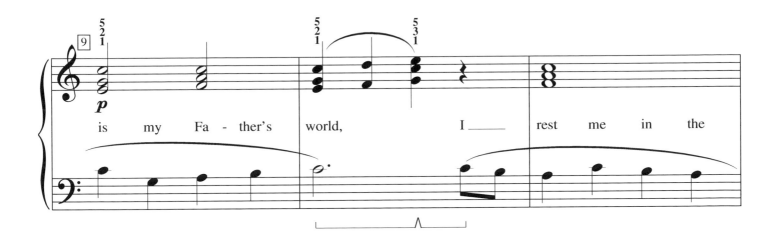

is my Fa - ther's world, I _____ rest me in the

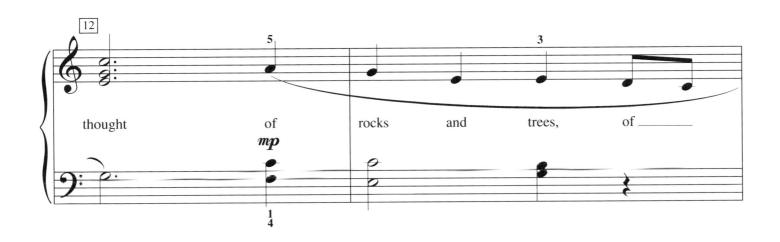

thought of rocks and trees, of _____

skies and seas. His hand _____ the won - ders _____ wrought.

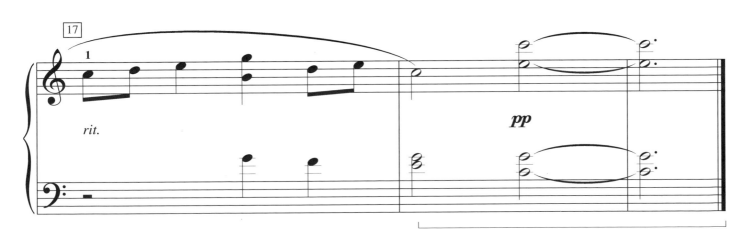

rit.

Eternal Father, Strong To Save

Words by William Whiting
Music by John Bacchus Dykes
Arranged by Phillip Keveren

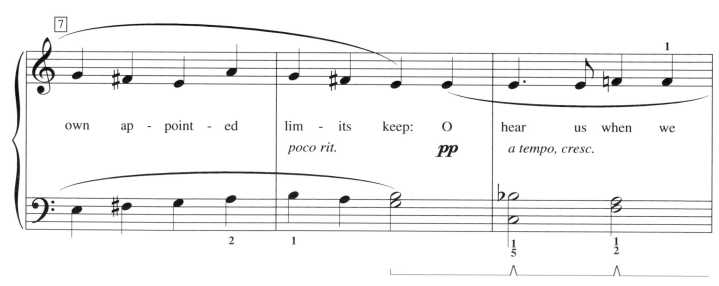

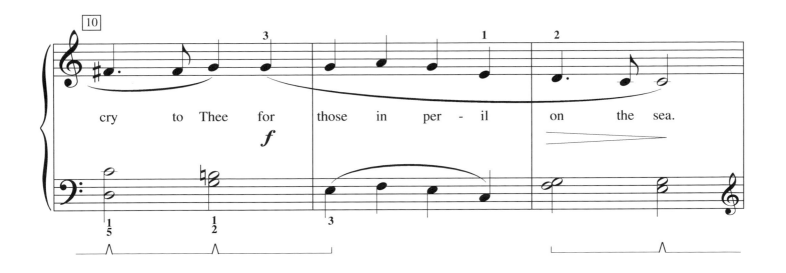

cry to Thee for those in per - il on the sea.

O Christ, the Lord of

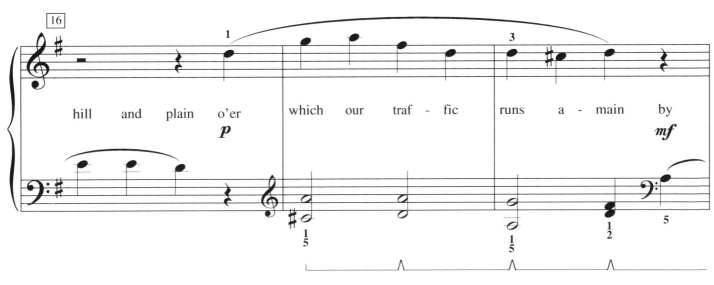

hill and plain o'er which our traf - fic runs a - main by

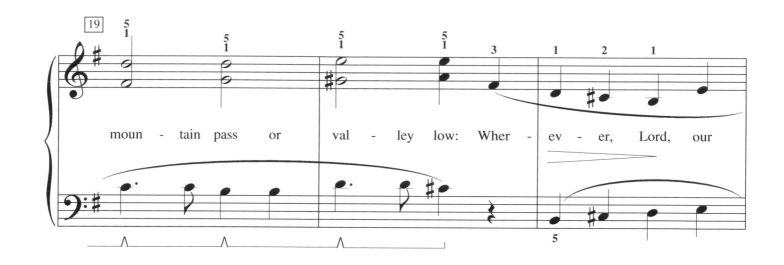

moun - tain pass or val - ley low: Wher - ev - er, Lord, our

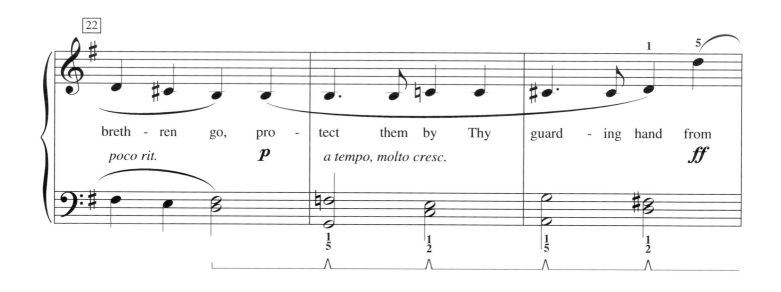

breth - ren go, pro - tect them by Thy guard - ing hand from

poco rit. *p* *a tempo, molto cresc.* *ff*

ev - 'ry per - il on the land.

molto rit. *mp*

Softly And Tenderly

Words and Music by Will L. Thompson
Arranged by Phillip Keveren

Andante (♩ = 100)

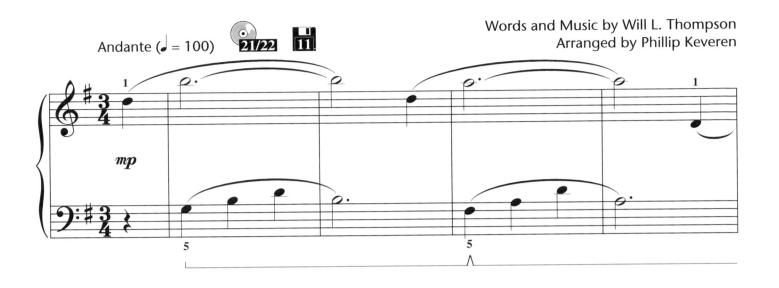

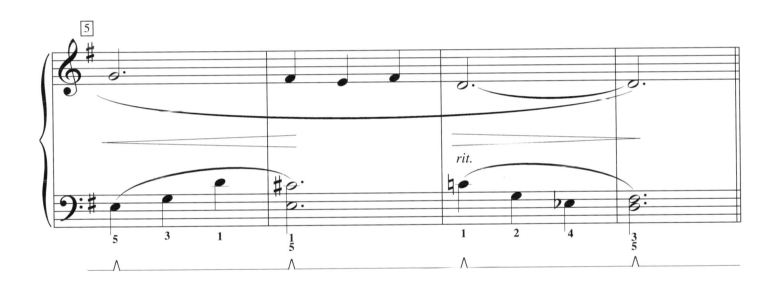

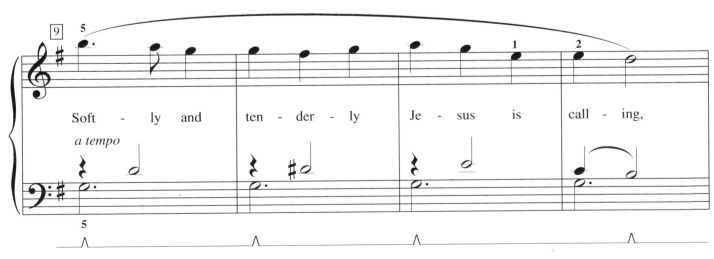

Soft - ly and ten - der - ly Je - sus is call - ing,

a tempo

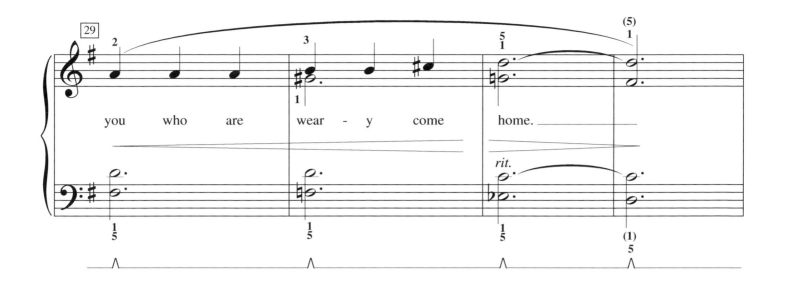

you who are wear - y come home.

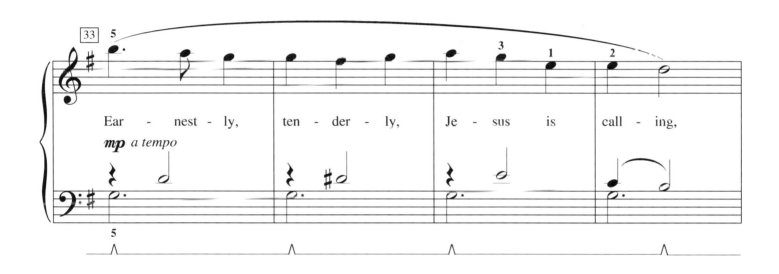

Ear - nest - ly, ten - der - ly, Je - sus is call - ing,

mp *a tempo*

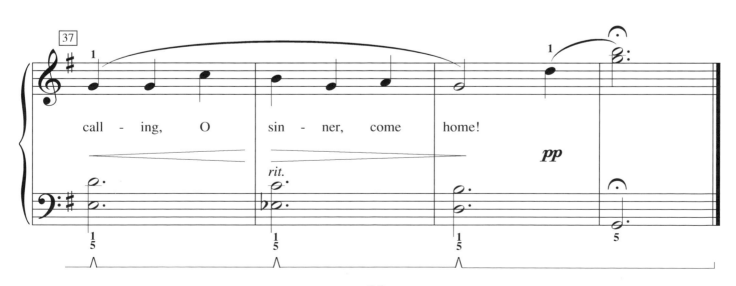

call - ing, O sin - ner, come home!

rit.

pp

Stand Up, Stand Up For Jesus

Words by George Duffield, Jr.
Music by George J. Webb
Arranged by Fred Kern

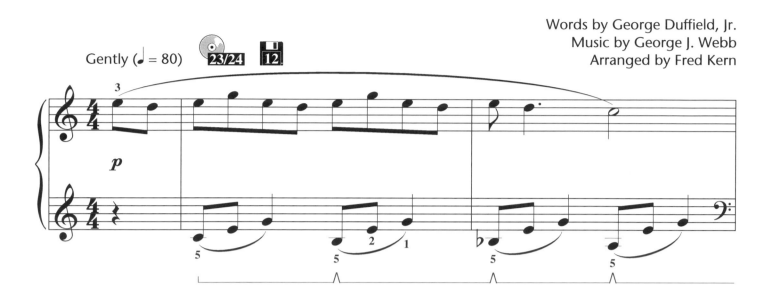

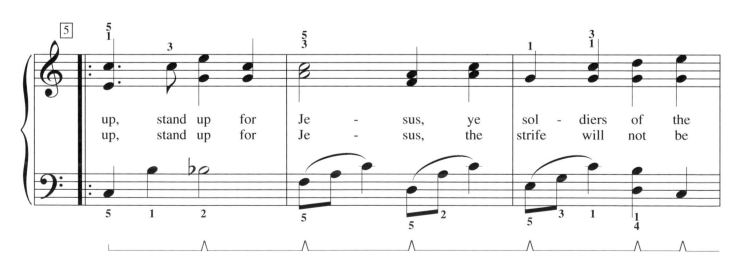

up, stand up for Je - sus, ye sol - diers of the
up, stand up for Je - sus, the strife will not be

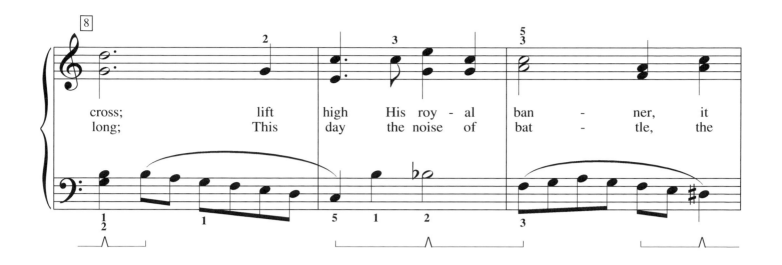

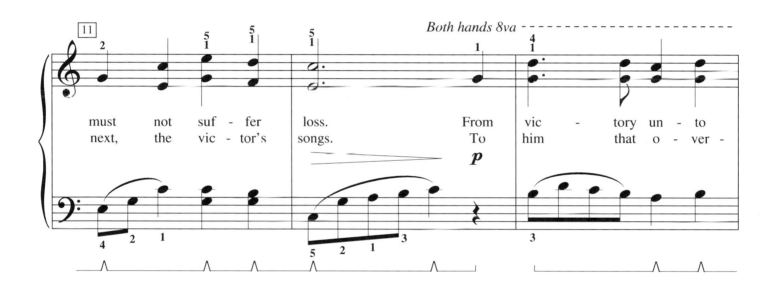

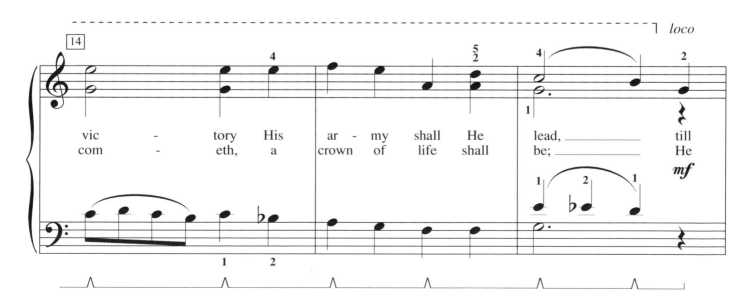

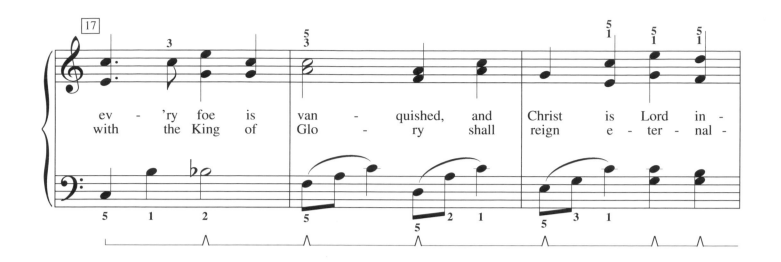

ev - 'ry foe is van - quished, and Christ is Lord in -
with the King of Glo - ry and shall reign e - ter - nal -

deed. Stand
ly.

mp

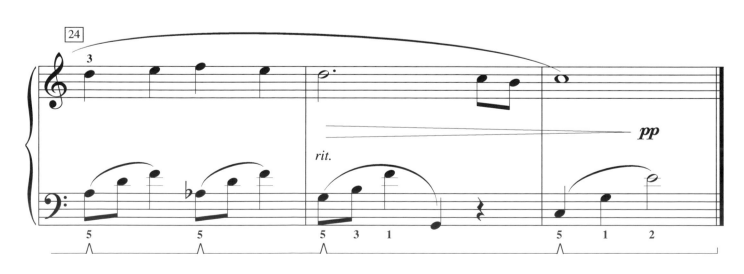

rit.

pp

Hal Leonard Student Piano Library

The *Hal Leonard Student Piano Library* has great music and solid pedagogy delivered in a truly creative and comprehensive method. It's that simple. A creative approach to learning using solid pedagogy and the best music produces skilled musicians! Great music means motivated students, inspired teachers and delighted parents. It's a method that encourages practice, progress, confidence, and best of all – success.

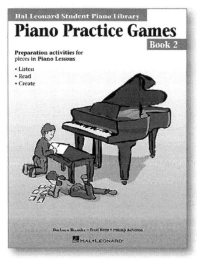

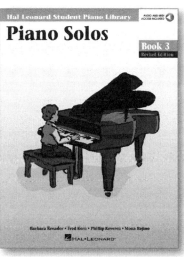

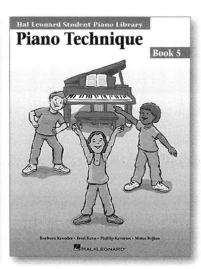

PIANO LESSONS BOOK 1
00296177 Book/Online Audio............................ $9.99
00296001 Book Only.. $7.99

PIANO PRACTICE GAMES BOOK 1
00296002 .... $7.99

PIANO SOLOS BOOK 1
00296568 Book/Online Audio............................ $9.99
00296003 Book Only.. $7.99

PIANO THEORY WORKBOOK BOOK 1
00296023 .... $7.50

PIANO TECHNIQUE BOOK 1
00296563 Book/Online Audio............................ $8.99
00296105 Book Only.. $7.99

NOTESPELLER FOR PIANO BOOK 1
00296088 .... $7.99

TEACHER'S GUIDE BOOK 1
00296048 .... $7.99

PIANO LESSONS BOOK 2
00296178 Book/Online Audio............................ $9.99
00296006 Book Only.. $7.99

PIANO PRACTICE GAMES BOOK 2
00296007 .... $8.99

PIANO SOLOS BOOK 2
00296569 Book/Online Audio............................ $8.99
00296008 Book Only.. $7.99

PIANO THEORY WORKBOOK BOOK 2
00296024 .... $7.99

PIANO TECHNIQUE BOOK 2
00296564 Book/Online Audio............................ $8.99
00296106 Book Only.. $7.99

NOTESPELLER FOR PIANO BOOK 2
00296089 .... $6.99

PIANO LESSONS BOOK 3
00296179 Book/Online Audio............................ $9.99
00296011 Book Only.. $7.99

PIANO PRACTICE GAMES BOOK 3
00296012 .... $7.99

PIANO SOLOS BOOK 3
00296570 Book/Online Audio............................ $8.99
00296013 Book Only.. $7.99

PIANO THEORY WORKBOOK BOOK 3
00296025 .... $7.99

PIANO TECHNIQUE BOOK 3
00296565 Book/Enhanced CD Pack.................. $8.99
00296114 Book Only.. $7.99

NOTESPELLER FOR PIANO BOOK 3
00296167 .... $7.99

PIANO LESSONS BOOK 4
00296180 Book/Online Audio............................ $9.99
00296026 Book Only.. $7.99

PIANO PRACTICE GAMES BOOK 4
00296027 .... $6.99

PIANO SOLOS BOOK 4
00296571 Book/Online Audio............................ $8.99
00296028 Book Only.. $7.99

PIANO THEORY WORKBOOK BOOK 4
00296038 .... $7.99

PIANO TECHNIQUE BOOK 4
00296566 Book/Online Audio............................ $8.99
00296115 Book Only.. $7.99

PIANO LESSONS BOOK 5
00296181 Book/Online Audio............................ $9.99
00296041 Book Only.. $8.99

PIANO SOLOS BOOK 5
00296572 Book/Online Audio............................ $9.99
00296043 Book Only.. $7.99

PIANO THEORY WORKBOOK BOOK 5
00296042 .... $8.99

PIANO TECHNIQUE BOOK 5
00296567 Book/Online Audio............................ $8.99
00296116 Book Only.. $8.99

ALL-IN-ONE PIANO LESSONS
00296761 Book A – Book/Online Audio $10.99
00296776 Book B – Book/Online Audio $10.99
00296851 Book C – Book/Online Audio $10.99
00296852 Book D – Book/Online Audio $10.99

Prices, contents, and availability subject to change without notice.

www.halleonard.com

The Best Sacred Collections for Piano

Blended Worship Piano Collection

Songs include: Amazing Grace (My Chains Are Gone) • Be Thou My Vision • I Will Rise • Joyful, Joyful, We Adore Thee • Lamb of God • Majesty • Open the Eyes of My Heart • Praise to the Lord, the Almighty • Shout to the Lord • 10,000 Reasons (Bless the Lord) • Worthy Is the Lamb • Your Name • and more.
00293528 Piano Solo $17.99

Hymn Anthology

A beautiful collection of 60 hymns arranged for piano solo, including: Abide with Me • Be Thou My Vision • Come, Thou Fount of Every Blessing • Doxology • For the Beauty of the Earth • God of Grace and God of Glory • Holy, Holy, Holy • It Is Well with My Soul • Joyful, Joyful, We Adore Thee • Let Us Break Bread Together • A Mighty Fortress Is Our God • O God, Our Help in Ages Past • Savior, like a Shepherd Lead Us • To God Be the Glory • What a Friend We Have in Jesus • and more.
00251244 Piano Solo $16.99

The Hymn Collection
arranged by Phillip Keveren

17 beloved hymns expertly and beautifully arranged for solo piano by Phillip Keveren. Includes: All Hail the Power of Jesus' Name • I Love to Tell the Story • I Surrender All • I've Got Peace Like a River • Were You There? • and more.
00311071 Piano Solo $14.99

Hymn Duets
arranged by Phillip Keveren

Includes lovely duet arrangements of: All Creatures of Our God and King • I Surrender All • It Is Well with My Soul • O Sacred Head, Now Wounded • Praise to the Lord, The Almighty • Rejoice, The Lord Is King • and more.
00311544 Piano Duet............................$14.99

Hymn Medleys
arranged by Phillip Keveren

Great medleys resonate with the human spirit, as do the truths in these moving hymns. Here Phillip Keveren combines 24 timeless favorites into eight lovely medleys for solo piano.
00311349 Piano Solo $14.99

P/V/G = Piano/Vocal/Guitar arrangements.

Prices, contents and availability subject to change without notice.

Hymns for Two
arranged by Carol Klose

12 piano duet arrangements of favorite hymns: Amazing Grace • Be Thou My Vision • Crown Him with Many Crowns • Fairest Lord Jesus • Holy, Holy, Holy • I Need Thee Every Hour • O Worship the King • What a Friend We Have in Jesus • and more.
00290544 Piano Duet............................$12.99

It Is Well
10 BELOVED HYMNS FOR MEMORIAL SERVICES
arr. John Purifoy

10 peaceful, soul-stirring hymn settings appropriate for memorial services and general worship use. Titles include: Abide with Me • Amazing Grace • Be Still My Soul • For All the Saints • His Eye Is on the Sparrow • In the Garden • It Is Well with My Soul • Like a River Glorious • Rock of Ages • What a Friend We Have in Jesus.
00118920 Piano Solo $12.99

Ragtime Gospel Classics
arr. Steven K. Tedesco

A dozen old-time gospel favorites: Because He Lives • Goodbye World Goodbye • He Touched Me • I Saw the Light • I'll Fly Away • Keep on the Firing Line • Mansion over the Hilltop • No One Ever Cared for Me like Jesus • There Will Be Peace in the Valley for Me • Victory in Jesus • What a Day That Will Be • Where Could I Go.
00142449 Piano Solo $11.99

Ragtime Gospel Hymns
arranged by Steven Tedesco

15 traditional gospel hymns, including: At Calvary • Footsteps of Jesus • Just a Closer Walk with Thee • Leaning on the Everlasting Arms • What a Friend We Have in Jesus • When We All Get to Heaven • and more.
00311763 Piano Solo $10.99

Sacred Classics for Solo Piano
arr. John Purifoy

10 timeless songs of faith, masterfully arranged by John Purifoy. Because He Lives • Easter Song • Glorify Thy Name • Here Am I, Send Me • I'd Rather Have Jesus • Majesty • On Eagle's Wings • There's Something About That Name • We Shall Behold Him • Worthy Is the Lamb.
00141703 Piano Solo $14.99

Raise Your Hands
PIANO SOLOS FOR BLENDED WORSHIP
arr. Heather Sorenson

10 uplifting and worshipful solos crafted by Heather Sorenson. Come Thou Fount, Come Thou King • God of Heaven • Holy Is the Lord (with "Holy, Holy, Holy") • Holy Spirit • I Will Rise • In Christ Alone • Raise Your Hands • Revelation Song • 10,000 Reasons (Bless the Lord) • Your Name (with "All Hail the Power of Jesus' Name").
00231579 Piano Solo $14.99

Seasonal Sunday Solos for Piano

24 blended selections grouped by occasion. Includes: Breath of Heaven (Mary's Song) • Come, Ye Thankful People, Come • Do You Hear What I Hear • God of Our Fathers • In the Name of the Lord • Mary, Did You Know? • Mighty to Save • Spirit of the Living God • The Wonderful Cross • and more.
00311971 Piano Solo $16.99

Sunday Solos for Piano

30 blended selections, perfect for the church pianist. Songs include: All Hail the Power of Jesus' Name • Be Thou My Vision • Great Is the Lord • Here I Am to Worship • Majesty • Open the Eyes of My Heart • and many more.
00311272 Piano Solo $17.99

More Sunday Solos for Piano

A follow-up to *Sunday Solos for Piano*, this collection features 30 more blended selections perfect for the church pianist. Includes: Agnus Dei • Come, Thou Fount of Every Blessing • The Heart of Worship • How Great Thou Art • Immortal, Invisible • O Worship the King • Shout to the Lord • Thy Word • We Fall Down • and more.
00311864 Piano Solo $16.99

Even More Sunday Solos for Piano

30 blended selections, including: Ancient Words • Brethren, We Have Met to Worship • How Great Is Our God • Lead On, O King Eternal • Offering • Savior, Like a Shepherd Lead Us • We Bow Down • Worthy of Worship • and more.
00312098 Piano Solo $16.99